Ulrich Renz · Marc Robitzky

야생의 백조

The Wild Swans

한스 크리스티안 안데르센 이중 언어 그림동화책

번역:

Lee Jin-Ho, Mannheim, Germany (한국어)

Ludwig Blohm and Pete Savill, Lübeck, Germany (영어)

옛날 옛적에 왕의 자녀 열두명이 살았는데 - 아들 열한명과
그들의누나 에리사 였습니다.

Once upon a time there were twelve royal children –
eleven brothers and one older sister, Elisa. They lived
happily in a beautiful castle.

어느날 어머니가 돌아가시고, 임금님은 다시 결혼을 하게
되었습니다. 하지만, 새 부인은 나쁜 마녀였죠. 그녀는 마법을 걸어
열한명의 왕자들을 백조로 변하게했고, 웅장한 숲을 넘어 아주 먼
나라로 보냈습니다.

One day the mother died, and some time later the king
married again. The new wife, however, was an evil witch.
She turned the eleven princes into swans and sent them far
away to a distant land beyond the large forest.

딸에게는 누더기옷을 입히고, 얼굴이 흉직해지는 약을 발라서, 아버지는 그녀를 더 이상 알아볼수가 없어, 왕궁에서 내쫓아 버렸습니다. 에리사는 어두운 숲속 안으로 뛰어 들어갔습니다.

She dressed the girl in rags and smeared an ointment onto her face that turned her so ugly, that even her own father no longer recognized her and chased her out of the castle. Elisa ran into the dark forest.

이제 그녀는 혼자가 되었고, 마음 속 깊은곳에는 사라져버린 형제들이 그리웠죠. 저녁이 되자, 나무 밑에 이끼로 침대를 만들었습니다.

Now she was all alone, and longed for her missing brothers from the depths of her soul. As the evening came, she made herself a bed of moss under the trees.

그 다음날 아침, 그녀는 조용한 호수가에 가서, 물위에 비친 자신의 얼굴을 보며 깜짝 놀랐습니다. 하지만 씻고 난 후에는, 태양 아래 제일 아름다운 공주였죠.

The next morning she came to a calm lake and was shocked when she saw her reflection in it. But once she had washed, she was the most beautiful princess under the sun.

여러 날들이 지나고 에리사는 큰 바다에 다다르게 되었습니다. 파도 위에는 열한개의 백조깃털이 둥둥 떠다녔습니다.

After many days Elisa reached the great sea. Eleven swan feathers were bobbing on the waves.

해가 지자 바람이 휭휭 불며, 백조 열한마리가 물위로 내려
앉았습니다. 에리사는 마법에 걸린 형제들을 바로 알아봤죠.
하지만 그들은 서로 백조들의 말로 얘기를 해서 그녀는 못
알아들었습니다.

As the sun set, there was a swooshing noise in the air and eleven wild swans landed on the water. Elisa immediately recognized her enchanted brothers. They spoke swan language and because of this she could not understand them.

낮엔 백조들이 먼곳으로 날아다니고, 밤엔 누나와 백조형제들이
동굴안에 서로 껴안으며 있었답니다.

어느날 밤, 에리사는 이상한 꿈을 꾸었습니다. 그 꿈에 어머니께서
형제들을 어떻게 구할수있는지 말씀하셨답니다. 쐐기풀로 백조들을
위해 각각 옷을 만들어, 그 위에 걸쳐 입히라고 했습니다. 그때까지는
말 한마디도 하면 않되고, 그것을 직히지 못할 경우 형재들은 모두
죽게된다고 했죠.
에리사는 그 일을 바로 시작했습니다. 그녀의 손은 불에 데이듯이
아파도, 지치지않고 옷을 계속 만들었습니다.

During the day the swans flew away, and at night the siblings
snuggled up together in a cave.

One night Elisa had a strange dream: Her mother told her how
she could release her brothers from the spell. She should knit
shirts from stinging nettles and throw one over each of the
swans. Until then, however, she was not allowed to speak a
word, or else her brothers would die.
Elisa set to work immediately. Although her hands were
burning as if they were on fire, she carried on knitting
tirelessly.

어느날 먼곳에서 사냥꾼의
나팔소리가 울렸습니다. 어느 왕자와
그의 호위병들이 말을타고 와, 곧
그녀앞에 서게되었습니다. 서로 눈이
마주치자마자 그들은 사랑에
빠졌습니다.

One day hunting horns sounded
in the distance. A prince came
riding along with his entourage
and he soon stood in front of her.
As they looked into each other's
eyes, they fell in love.

왕자는 에리사를 말위에 같이 태워
그의 성으로 데려갔습니다.

The prince lifted Elisa onto his
horse and rode to his castle with
her.

권력있는 금고지기는 말을 못하고
아름다운 그녀가 오는것을 전혀
좋아하지 않았습니다. 자신의 딸이
왕자의 신부가 되길
원했기때문이였죠.

The mighty treasurer was
anything but pleased with the
arrival of the silent beauty. His
own daughter was meant to
become the prince's bride.

에리사는 그녀의 형제들을 잊지
않았습니다. 매일 저녁 계속 옷을
만들었답니다. 어느날 밤, 에리사는
새로운 쐐기풀을 구하러 무덤가로
갔습니다. 금고지기는 그녀를 몰래
지켜보고 있었죠.

Elisa had not forgotten her
brothers. Every evening she
continued working on the shirts.
One night she went out to the
cemetery to gather fresh nettles.
While doing so she was secretly
watched by the treasurer.

왕자님이 사냥을 하러 떠나자, 금고지기는 에리사를 감옥에 가둬놓았습니다. 그녀가 마녀이고 밤에는 다른 마녀들을 만난다고 말을 했답니다.

As soon as the prince was away on a hunting trip, the treasurer had Elisa thrown into the dungeon. He claimed that she was a witch who met with other witches at night.

새벽에 경비병들이 에리사를 끌고
갔습니다. 그녀를 시장광장에서
태우려고 했습니다.

At dawn, Elisa was fetched by the
guards. She was going to be
burned to death at the
marketplace.

그녀가 장소에 도착하자 마자, 갑자기 열한마리의 백조들이
날아왔습니다. 에리사는 얼른 모든 백조에게 쐐기풀옷을 던져
입혔습니다. 바로 그녀의 형재들이 모두 사람의 모습으로 그녀
앞에 나타났죠. 제일 막내 혼자만, 옷이 끝까지 완성되지 못해,
한쪽팔 대신 날개가 남아 있었답니다.

No sooner had she arrived there, when suddenly eleven white swans came flying towards her. Elisa quickly threw a shirt over each of them. Shortly thereafter all her brothers stood before her in human form. Only the smallest, whose shirt had not been quite finished, still had a wing in place of one arm.

형제들은 아직 계속 부등켜 안고 서로 기뻐하고 있을때,
왕자님께서는 돌아왔습니다. 에리사는 드디어 그에게 모든 것을
설명할 수 있었습니다. 왕자님께서는 나쁜 금고지기를 감옥에
가둬버렸답니다. 그 후 칠일 동안 혼인잔치를 했습니다.

그리고 모두 모두 행복하게 살았답니다.

The siblings' joyous hugging and kissing hadn't yet finished
as the prince returned. At last Elisa could explain everything
to him. The prince had the evil treasurer thrown into the
dungeon. And after that the wedding was celebrated for
seven days.

And they all lived happily ever after.

Children's Books for the Global Village

Ever more children are born away from their parents' home countries, and are balancing between the languages of their mother, their father, their grandparents, and their peers. Our bilingual books are meant to help bridge the language divides that cross more and more families, neighborhoods and kindergartens in the globalized world.

The Wild Swans also propose to you:

Sleep Tight, Little Wolf

► A heart-warming bedtime story for sleepy children (and their sleepy parents)
► Reading age 2 and up
► Available in more than 60 languages

www.childrens-books-bilingual.com

NEW! Little Wolf in Sign Language

Home	Authors	Little Wolf	About

Bilingual Children's Books - in any language you want

Welcome to Little Wolf's Language Wizard!

Just choose the two languages in which you want to read to your children:

Language 1:

French ⌄

Language 2:

Icelandic ⌄

Go!

Learn more about our bilingual books at www.childrens-books-bilingual.com. At the heart of this website you will find what we call our "Language Wizard". It contains more than 60 languages and any of their bilingual combinations: Just select, in a simple drop-down-menu, the two languages in which you'd like to read "Little Wolf" or "The Wild Swans" to your child – and the book is instantly made available, ready for order as an ebook download or as a printed edition.

Hans Christian Andersen was born in the Danish city of Odense in 1805, and died in 1875 in Copenhagen. He gained world fame with his fairy-tales such as "The Little Mermaid", "The Emperor's New Clothes" and "The Ugly Duckling". The tale at hand, "The Wild Swans", was first published in 1838. It has been translated into more than one hundred languages and adapted for a wide range of media including theater, film and musical.

Ulrich Renz was born in Stuttgart, Germany, in 1960. After studying French literature in Paris he graduated from medical school in Lübeck and worked as head of a scientific publishing company. He is now a writer of non-fiction books as well as children's fiction books. www.ulrichrenz.de

Marc Robitzky, born in 1973, studied at the Technical School of Art in Hamburg and the Academy of Visual Arts in Frankfurt. He works as a freelance illustrator and communication designer in Aschaffenburg (Germany). www.robitzky.eu

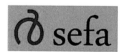

Made in the USA
San Bernardino, CA
21 August 2017